THE ECONOMIC PROBLEM
IN PEACE AND WAR

THE ECONOMIC PROBLEM
IN PEACE AND WAR

*Some Reflections on Objectives
and Mechanisms*

BY

LIONEL ROBBINS

PROFESSOR OF ECONOMICS IN
THE UNIVERSITY OF LONDON

LONDON
MACMILLAN & CO. LTD
1947

FOREWORD

THE following lectures were given at Cambridge on the Marshall foundation in the spring of this year. In preparing them for publication, I have made no attempt to disguise the fact that they were written to be spoken aloud. Save for purely stylistic corrections and the insertion of a few sentences here and there, designed to relieve undue compression or to reinforce a point, they remain as they were delivered. I should like to take this opportunity of thanking the members of the Economics Faculty at Cambridge for their friendly invitation and for the great kindness which they showed to a very imperfect lecturer.

LIONEL ROBBINS

THE LONDON SCHOOL OF ECONOMICS
May 1947

CONTENTS

THE MECHANISMS OF DISTRIBUTION AND THE OBJECTIVES OF PRODUCTION

1. *Purpose of the Lectures*

WHEN your Faculty Board was so kind as to invite me to deliver these lectures, I am afraid I accepted in a very unreflecting spirit. To appear, so to speak, under the auspices of the great founder of your tradition is a privilege which perhaps few of us would be strong-minded enough to refuse. But when I came to consider the responsibilities which I had assumed, I confess I became somewhat alarmed. For six years I had been engaged in non-academic pursuits. For the last year I had been engaged in a painful effort at re-education — I can now just begin to trust myself to put a curve on the board and to engage in mild altercation with my friends who are in better training. But that, at this stage of my intellectual re-conversion, I should put before you theoretical novelties and new analytical constructions was unthinkable ; I should be disgraced, and you would be bored, by the venture. Yet the other obvious alternative, that I should choose as my theme some special episode of the economic history of the war with which I had had some acquaintance, was almost equally unattractive. I would not wish to delay my own re-education by living too much in the past. You would not wish to hear me retell, from perhaps a slightly different point of view, incidents which, in their main outlines, have already become part and parcel of the staple courses in contemporary economic history.

Eventually I came to the conclusion that the difficulty might in part be met if I addressed myself to considerations of a rather broader nature. The war has cut some of us off from opportunities of research and speculation. But this discontinuity has not been without some compensating advantages. It has afforded insights into the physiology of the body economic in conditions of unusual strain. It has offered opportunities of putting some, at least, of our beliefs to the test of fact. It has afforded an interval in which, our entanglement in the controversies of the past being suspended, we could reconsider old positions without that acute attachment to already invested intellectual capital, which, in normal times, makes it so difficult to change one's position. To-day, freed from the pressure of day-to-day business and the limitations of official discretion, we find ourselves confronted once more with the necessity of establishing a general perspective. Might it not, therefore, be worth while to seize this opportunity of continuing, so to speak, the process of self-re-education in public and to ask where we stand to-day on some of the broader questions. To what extent has the experience of war confirmed, to what extent has it enlarged or confounded our beliefs concerning what economic policy can do for the advancement of human welfare? To tackle such questions broadside on, in the form of systematic analysis, would be unbearably pretentious, even if, in the space of three lectures, it were not physically impracticable. But to proceed by way of reflection and reformulation in the light of recent experience and present problems might perhaps offer a method of approach which would make the problem much more manageable.

That, at any rate, is the method which I intend to pursue in these lectures. I propose to put to myself, as it were, some of the larger questions of economic policy and to ask: to what extent have my views on these matters been modified or confirmed by the experience of war; to what extent do the needs of the contemporary situation call for reformulation or reaffirmation of doctrines to which in the past I have been led to attach importance? In my first lecture, I propose to discuss some of the basic objectives of production and distribution; in the second, the rationale of the war economy and its applicability to the problems of transition and peace; in the third, a mode of approach to the problems of planning and control in peace-time which seems to me more in harmony with the findings of economic analysis and the requirements of a free society.

Let me try to make a little more precise the thought which has been at the back of my mind in preparing these lectures for delivery. Those of us who became economists in the inter-war period were brought up upon textbooks which purported to furnish an explanation of the economic system of the day : and one of the central preoccupations of these works was the nature and functions of price. In a system based predominantly on private property and the division of labour, the price system, we were taught, served three main purposes : to secure the distribution of given goods ; to indicate the preferences of the citizens concerning what goods should be produced in the future ; and to provide a stimulus and a guide to the organization of production. We have lived through a period in which the operation of price and the price system has been, to a large extent, suspended. We are living in a period in which many doubts prevail concerning the part which private property and the market have to play in the organization of production. What light has this experience to throw upon the doctrines of the past ? What place in our general perspective should be occupied by the controversies about organization ? It is this kind of problem to which I shall be trying to formulate some broad indication of attitude. In all that I have to say I shall be concerned only with the most general questions of principle ; save for digressions and illustrations, I shall not touch at all upon detailed problems. In particular, I shall refrain almost altogether from international applications, although in practice in the next few years these are likely to occupy the foreground of attention. There is much that I should like to say about these things. But I conceive that for an academic economist the first duty in any intellectual stocktaking is to make sure where he stands on the broadest fundamentals. There will always be plenty of others only too ready to proceed from the *ad hoc* to the general.

2. *The Mechanism of Distribution*

I turn first to the function of price as a means for distributing given goods. Here what I have to say will be reasonably brief. For, in this connection at least, I am inclined to think that the experience of war vindicates completely the doctrine of the textbooks, namely, that with *given* goods and a *given* distribution of income and capital — please note this second qualification — there is nothing like the market mechanism for getting the goods into, roughly speaking, the right hands.

At first sight this may seem unbearably paradoxical. For, with the outbreak of war and the consequential development of severe scarcities, we abandoned free prices and went over to rationing on a large scale. Nor, in my judgment, was this policy without complete justification, both in the needs of the situation and in the tradition of classical political economy. From the time of David Hume onwards, economists have held that conditions of siege justified the imposition of rationing; and, in the recent six years' siege some of us devoted much time to devising new methods of carrying out the classical prescription.

But the reason for this lay, not in any deficiency of the price system as a means of distributing given goods with given incomes, but rather in the universally held conviction that, in conditions of siege, the initial distribution of purchasing power operating through the market would have resulted in an unsatisfactory distribution of goods. A free price would have cleared the market. With free prices there would have been no queues and no shop shortages. But the superior power to demand of those with relatively higher incomes and capital, including, do not let us forget, the better paid wage earners, would have left too little available for those at the bottom of the scale; and since it was not deemed practicable to carry taxation to the point at which the distribution of power to demand approximated to the condition of equality considered equitably appropriate to a siege, supplementary measures had to be adopted. It was not the price system as such which was wrong, it was the initial distribution of money. If the distribution of income and property had happened to correspond to what for the time being was considered equitable, then the only argument for rationing would have been the belief that, in the special conditions prevailing, people did not know what was best for them or for the children for whom they were responsible.

But this is not the only moral to be learnt from the war experience. It was not possible to go very far with the traditional methods of rationing before their limitations, as compared with the price system, became very painfully apparent. Where you are dealing with commodities which are easily standardized and which are in universal demand — margarine, tea, bacon, for example — the adoption of single-line rationing, on a completely egalitarian basis, or upon very simple classifications of assumed need, does not work very badly. Even here, of course, tastes differ; some may get more, and some less, than they would upon an all-wise allocation according to need. On the whole, however, the system does achieve rough justice. But as soon as you get beyond this, into the realm of commodities which are less capable of standardization, and which are the object of more varying needs and tastes, it becomes completely inapplicable. A uniform ration of trousers or tinned fruit would be absurd. As you all know, it was to meet these difficulties that point rationing was adopted.

But what was this but the re-establishment, at least on the demand side, of the essential features of the price system? Point values are prices, point allotments cash. The difference was solely that the initial distribution of power to demand was different. And despite the scepticism of those to whom the elementary laws of supply and demand had all the unacceptability of new truth, the system did what was expected of it. It has not always worked perfectly. The fact that, on the supply side, points are not in every respect the same as money and that there is no incentive in the shape of point profits to move goods without direction, precludes the attainment of the full automatism of the price system. But such imperfections as have developed on the demand side have all sprung from unwillingness to use the mechanism sufficiently vigorously — the reluctance of public officials to change prices is an interesting sociological phenomenon. When the system has been worked as it should be, it has satisfied all expectations.

Now the moral I draw from all this is very simple. There is nothing wrong with the market as such as a mechanism for distributing goods; quite the contrary indeed. The objections, such as they are, apply not to the market, but to the configuration of power to demand to which the market responds. Hence I should argue as a normal rule — I make no generalization on war emergencies — that, if it is felt that the working of the market results in a distribution of goods which is not equitable, the remedy is to be found, not in suspending the market or in falsifying the system of prices, but rather in direct operation on the level of net incomes and property either by way of taxation or by way of sub-sidies to persons. If it is thought that the rich get too much, then they should be taxed. If it is thought that the prices of essential commodities are too high for the pockets of the lowest group of income receivers, then give them money. Or if it is felt that the poorest con-sumers are so silly or so irresponsible that they cannot spend increased money incomes properly either for them-selves or (what is more important) for their children, then give them income in kind, as in the free milk schemes. But do not throw the baby out with the bath-water by suspending the market or by fixing prices below the point of market equilibrium. That way lies frustration and much economic waste.

If I might divagate, for one moment, into questions of contemporary policy, I would say that this conclusion has a very urgent application to our present condition. It is true that we are not yet out of the wood of quasi-siege conditions; we must not judge too harshly the *ad hoc* arrangements of the transition. But it is also true that we are in a condition in which it is more than usually desirable that full scope should be given to the operation of cash incentive. And, as I see it, we are following a policy which is self-contradictory and self-frustrating. We are relaxing taxation and seeking, wherever possible, to introduce systems of payments which fluctuate with output. And, at the same time, our price fixing and the consequential rationing systems are inspired by egalitarian principles. The result is that we get the worst of both worlds. We suffer the inconveniences of rationing and shop shortages and we do not get the incentive effect of inequalities of payment. I cannot believe that, in the long run, this is a good plan. Let us by all means seek to prevent hardship and gross inequality; my Utopia as regards the national minimum income lies quite as far to the left as most of you would regard as desirable. But let us do this *via* taxation and income from civil rights (*i.e.* family allowances and the like) rather than muddle about with systems of artificial prices which are grossly wasteful, which frustrate incentive and which

9   B

make it progressively more difficult to get into anything like equilibrium.

3. *Objectives of Production*

I now turn to what, I submit, is a much more interesting, because more controversial, aspect of the price system — its function, not as a means of distributing given goods but as a means for deciding what goods should be produced in the future. To what extent do we still agree that it is a good thing, that, the distribution of capital and income being given, production should be directed by reference to anticipated demand? Note please that I am not asking how production should be managed, whether it should be on a basis of private or public enterprise or some mixture of these principles. I am asking whether it is the consumers' choice which should rule or some other criterion. The question of organization is analytically quite distinct from the question of objectives; and, although I shall have a good deal to say about it later on, it is essential to the deployment of my argument that it should be kept quite separate at this stage. For the whole of this lecture, if it helps you to keep calm, you may imagine that I am discussing the criteria of policy in a completely collectivist community.

To establish a sense of proportion and to provide a basis for comparison in this connection, it is desirable to realize that in no circumstances are all goods chosen through the market. Even in the profoundest times of peace and in the most laissez-faire of free economies there is an important group of goods, the so-called public goods, which are chosen another way. Roads, lighthouses, the apparatus of collective sanitation, parks, public museums are examples of this class, the distinguishing feature of which is that the benefits are *indiscriminate* and consequently *cannot* be chosen on the basis of individual price bidding. Security is another such good; from the analytical point of view, as I shall be arguing next time, one of the most salient characteristics of the war economy is a vast extension of the production of goods for the provision of this kind of benefit.

Now there are two aspects of the processes whereby these goods are chosen which are highly significant when contrasted with the operation of the price system.

In the first place, they involve the overriding of minorities. Be the method of decision never so democratic, then, save in the limiting case of unanimity, there must always be those who vote *for* such production and those who vote *against*. There are those who think the satisfaction to themselves (or to others) worth what they will have to give up; and there are those who are of the contrary opinion. But, once the decision is taken, the negative votes are ignored. The arterial road is built, and those who did not want it can use it or not as they please; in any case, they pay the taxes. There is, so to speak, in all this an irreducible element of coercion — the difference between a tax and a purchase price.

In the second place, if we consider these decisions

realistically, we must recognize that, with the most democratic political machinery conceivable, it is stretching language very far indeed to speak as if the mechanism of particular decisions was, in fact, democratic. It is perhaps possible to conceive that in a small governmental area, a town borough, for instance, there might be an election solely devoted to a proposal to make a park; in which case, if they were told of the costs involved as well as of benefits promised, the electorate might truly be said to decide for or against. But in the majority of cases this is not possible. There is not one, there is a number of such projects to be decided upon, with a much greater number of alternative aspects of expenditure; and decision by election is unthinkable. In any case, most national elections are fought about other issues. The result is that the actual decisions are not made by the electorate at all but by bodies of ministers or officials, who may or may not be paying much attention to nice shades of desirability to the public. The most that can be hoped of democratic control in such cases is that questions may be asked in Parliament; and, if decisions are very flagrantly unpopular, they may become the subject of retrospective censure at subsequent elections — if nothing more important happens to be on the *tapis*, which perhaps is not very often.

Contrast what happens when goods — private goods, we may call them — are called into being through the market.

In the first place, there need be no overriding of

minorities. The sums in the hands of the consumers are, so to speak, proportionate claims on the services of the factors of production. Within the limits of these claims any idiosyncrasy may be satisfied. If a factor of production is in great demand in one use, the amount which may have to be spent to command its services in other uses will be greater than otherwise would be the case. But, provided the consumers are willing to pay, they may have it where they will. No one is compelled to buy what he does not want. Individual payments are at least proportionate to individual benefit.

In the second place, the ultimate control must rest with those who are immediately concerned with use or enjoyment. Now, of course, it is not true, as some have incautiously claimed, that even under the most perfect market system, consumers decide *directly* what shall be produced in the future. That decision is the business of the immediate controllers of production ; and it is a most important question of policy to determine what rules and mechanisms are most appropriate to make these decisions conform to the probable requirements of the consumers. But, assuming for the purposes of this argument that that question has been settled, assuming that we have a competitive order, corrected, if you will, by judicious taxes and subsidies, or a collectivist order run according to the rules of Lange or Lerner — or some improved system — then although the consumers do not make the immediate decisions, they will, so to speak, have continuous right of veto. The producers will decide in anticipation of demand. But the consumers will decide whether the anticipations were correct. Whatever may be the actual deficiencies of the market on the supply side, it is certainly capable, on the demand side, of providing, as it were, a process of election which not only allows proportionate registration of minority opinion, but also provides for continuous review of producers' decisions by those most immediately concerned with their ultimate results.

At once I want to guard against a possible misunderstanding. In making these comparisons between the mechanisms available for choosing different kinds of goods, I am not seeking to prejudice you against public goods as such. I should no more question the necessity of some public goods than the necessity of the state itself. To remove all doubt, let me say explicitly that I suspect that at the present time there is considerably more need for public goods than it has been customary to assume in the past; we can probably do with a good deal more indiscriminate benefit. But at the same time I would argue — and this, of course, is the real reason for my comparisons — that where there exists the possibility of an apparatus of choice, not involving the overriding of minorities and more directly responsive to individual preferences, then there seems to be a *prima facie* case in its favour. It is not to deny extensive and important functions to the state or ample scope for the production of public goods, to argue that, if there exists a method of putting the ultimate decision regarding private goods in the hands of those who enjoy them, rather than having recourse to the more indirect methods necessary elsewhere, the presumption is in favour of using it. I would argue this, not merely on grounds of consumers' utility, but also on grounds of efficiency of the political mechanism.

It is not such a very long time ago that such a conclusion would have been fairly generally accepted — at any rate in the main centres of western civilization. But in our own day, partly because of war which necessarily puts the individual at a discount, partly because of the popularity of schemes for over-all collectivist control of production, which carry with them a certain bias towards the standardization of consumption, it has come under strong criticism. Some of this criticism seems to me to be fundamentally unacceptable, some to point to real *lacunae* in the traditional analysis. In any case, I think it may be useful to examine what is said. In doing this I must ask you once again to bear in mind that what is under discussion is, not the reaction of different supply mechanisms to given consumers' preferences, but consumers' preference as expressed in the market as a criterion for judging the effectiveness of different types of supply.

I do not think we need waste much time on the complaint that the choice of goods on this principle involves the production of luxuries before necessities, cigars before calories, cars before cottages, etc. etc. This argument, although very popular, clearly rests on a confusion between the price system considered as a mechanism and the distribution of income to which it may be made to respond. I hope that what I have said already sufficiently covers this matter. If you think that incomes should be completely equal or proportionate to some conventional conception of need, well and good. That is no argument against allowing the citizens to bid for what they wish with their incomes, and taking these bids as the criterion of what should be produced. If, as is more probable, you hold that, for reasons of incentive and perhaps of decentralization of initiative and power, some differentiation is necessary, then you must not grumble if the market transforms inequality of net money incomes into inequality of real incomes. The belief that, in normal times, it is particularly sensible to try to mix the principles and to run an egalitarian real income system side by side with an inegalitarian money income system seems to me somewhat *simpliste*. You can do it on special occasions. But if you try to make it the regular plan you are likely to run into difficulties. You can fool some of the people some of the time. But that is about the limit.

Much more formidable is the argument that people do not know what is good for them and that therefore a system which chooses private goods on a basis of individual choice is likely to lead to less happiness or less well-being, than one which is based upon wise prescriptions from above. This is the well-known attitude of paternalism. We all know the imposing apparatus of pleading by which it has been supported. At the one end are attempted demonstrations of the supposedly bad results of specific choices; at the other, metaphysical arguments that in an apparatus of constraint is to be

16

found the basis of more perfect freedom, realization of the best self, attainment of true liberty and so on and so forth. . . .

Now in the workaday life of this world it is important not to be doctrinaire. I imagine we should all be prepared to admit that many bad results may follow from the ignorance of consumers, though, in the majority of cases, it is easy to think of better ways of remedying this than a general suspension of freedom. Education, the requirement of proper labelling of bottles, the enforcement of public tests of quality and safety, and, occasionally, indirect taxes and subsidies — these are measures of correction not usually regarded as inappropriate to a free society. We should all agree, too, to the proper protection of minors. A reasonable belief in freedom for adults does not imply complete freedom for the occupants of the cradle.

But considerations of this sort do not really touch the heart of the issue. It is not a question of what measures are to be taken in order that consumers may know the technical nature of what they are choosing. Nor is it a question of what restraints are to be placed upon children. The question is rather what is to be done about choice which is *not* the victim of technical ignorance or obvious fraud. What is to be done about the choices of people who are *not* minors? And here I think the lines of distinction, although sometimes blurred by sophistry, are really very clear in essence. Do we believe in control by consumers or do we not?

On this, although I am very far from desiring to under-estimate the weight of the sincere arguments which can be adduced on the side of paternalism, my own convictions are very definite. I hold that there is an essential arrogance — a sin of pride if you wish — in believing that we are so competent to decide for others the way of life they should follow that we should wish to assume to ourselves compulsory powers of control. And I hold too — you may regard it as even more of a superstition — that no choice can be regarded as having much ethical value if it is not in some sense free. I do not agree with many of the preferences of my fellow citizens. I yield to no one the right to describe them as silly, vulgar, self-frustrating, even wrong, if you wish to use that sort of language. But I hold that these are matters for argument and persuasion rather than coercion ; and that, although there is no guarantee in the nature of things that the free society will also be a good society, yet that it is somehow in the nature of things that only a society which has freedom in this sense can ever hope to achieve that which is good. That is to say, good government is no substitute for self-government and it is an essential function of the state to make as much self-government as possible available.

But now I come to an argument which, from our point of view as economists, is much more interesting and in some respects even more important — an argument which rests upon the denial of the sharp line which I have been drawing between the public goods which cannot be chosen by means of a market and the private goods which can.

Granted, it is said, that in the case of goods where the benefit of consumption is purely private, there may exist a presumption in favour of individual choice, yet there are also goods of a more mixed nature where there is, so to speak, a considerable penumbra of indiscriminate benefit or detriment associated with private consumption. You may bid for these goods on an estimate of the difference which they make to your private enjoyment. But the addition to the sum-total of enjoyment associated with their use is either greater or less than this; and your calculation leaves out these other elements altogether. This analysis no doubt is familiar to many of you — like most alleged novelties, it is to be found in that great book *The Economics of Welfare*. It is parallel in type to the analysis which draws our attention to the external economies and diseconomies of production; indeed the indiscriminate benefits and damages which it reveals have been called the external economies and diseconomies of consumption.

Now from a formal point of view, so far as I can see, this analysis is incontestable; and I can think of at least one case where it has implications which, in my judgment, are very important for practice. I refer to the uncontrolled development of real property. Here is a pleasant hillside. If you pay, you can procure a plot and induce a builder to erect for you an agreeable dwelling. What could be more delightful? But if, at the same time, other consumers are moved by the same impulse, the result is insensibly changed. The total picture, which affects your enjoyment and theirs, never comes into the market; and the end product may easily be something in which the quality of enjoyment is substantially lower than might easily have been the case if collective forethought had paid some attention, not so much to the design of the buildings — I have some suspicions of official architects — but at least to the layout of plots and road facilities. An apparatus of choice which is focussed entirely on discriminate benefit, to the neglect of what is indiscriminate, may thus easily leave out here something which is vitally significant for the texture and tone of daily life. Who can look at the shambles which is Greater London to-day, without acknowledging that with all the increase in private happiness which has come from this proliferation of villadom — and the increase is very real — something quite fundamental has been forgotten.

But, important as this argument may be in particular cases, it is easy to see how frightfully it may be abused as a justification for general paternalism. There is scarcely anything which I can do outside the privacy of my home which has not some overtone of indiscriminate benefit or detriment. The clothes I wear, the shows I frequent, the flowers that I plant in my garden, all directly, or through the mysterious influence of fashion, influence the enjoyments and satisfactions of others. Even what is done remote from the perception of others can be conceived to have this aspect. The fact that other people lead a way of life different from my own, that they like and buy pictures and books of which I disapprove and give private banquets of sacred meat and forbidden wines, can clearly be the occasion to me of most intense mortification. Is this to be included in the calculus of external economies and diseconomies? I can think of few forms of totalitarian regimentation of consumption which could not find some formal justification by appeal to this analysis. It is no accident that the Hegelian philosophers, whose methodical sapping of the intellectual foundations of liberty has been responsible for so many of the evils of our day, always made a bee-line for Mill's useful distinction between self-regarding and other regarding actions, and concentrated all the acid of their anti-libertarian hatreds upon dissolving the core of good sense underlying this useful, if not perhaps perfectly phrased, distinction.

Hence I would urge that we must be very watchful. We must not let our distrust of paternalism blind us to the real importance of some special cases which this analysis helps us to understand. But we must be ever on the alert against letting formal analysis without concrete investigation be made the pretext for undervaluing institutions which have an important part to play in the life of a free society. We must realize that too much stress on the penumbra of indiscriminate benefit may easily lead us to ignore the solid core of benefit which is discriminate. And if the exponents of totalitarian methods try to rush us with vague and unproved generalizations about " the values of social life as a pattern " and the mystic joys of tribal unity, we must be prepared to come back with an insistence that variety and spontaneity are also collective values which the wise man will hesitate to jeopardize.

All this of course is a matter of opinion concerning ultimate values far beyond the scope of the kind of analysis with which I am principally concerned. But of one thing we can be tolerably certain. The market is a vigorous institution, capable of adapting itself to many changes of public policy expressed in taxes, subsidies, particular prohibitions, general regulations and the like, and still continuing to perform its essential function of registering the preferences of the consumers spending their incomes within this framework. But any attempt to supersede the market on a grand scale and to substitute other values as a basis for controlling production must necessarily bring about an almost total change in the relation between the individual and society as we have hitherto known it in times of peace. Where private goods are chosen on the same basis as public goods, there the response of the productive organization to individual wants and fancies necessarily becomes so attenuated as for all practical purposes to be non-existent — instead of the daily market, the quinquennial election; instead of the detailed vote on individual goods, the total plan on a take-it-or-leave-it basis.

It is here I think that experience in time of war of the mechanisms whereby the kinds and quantities to be produced are actually chosen in such a system, gives a more vivid sense of the differences involved than any amount of imaginative speculation. Our theories of state action usually imply, not merely infinite wisdom on the part of administrators, but also infinite time in which to use it. It is not until you have sat in the smoke-filled committee rooms working against time to get snap decisions from Ministers who, through no fault of their own, are otherwise preoccupied, that you realize sufficiently the limitations of these assumptions. Nor are the more fundamental of these limitations removable by improvements of organization. You may reform your system of ministerial committees. You may augment the number of their advisers. You may employ troops of investigators to ascertain the reactions of consumers. You may stretch the sympathetic imagination to the utmost to seek to provide, within the limits of your plan, the kind of variety which you conceive to be desirable. You may sincerely believe that the process as you work it is, in some sense, good for the people. But I cannot think that, if you are honest with yourself, you can believe that such a system involves, or can involve, such degree of freedom for the consumer to get what he wishes, such an active participation in the daily moulding of social life, as a system which is based upon demand prices. The word democracy is so variously used nowadays that it is perhaps futile to discuss the question whether the approval of a total quantitative plan, not based upon market values, is or is not democratic. But it is very clearly skies apart from a system — whether socialist or individualist does not matter — which does follow the market. I have no doubt that some at least of those who talk broadly of the acceptance in will and understanding of the plan by the people sincerely believe that their words have some meaning. But I personally find it hard to believe that the process of choice thus conceived, with its apparatus of high-pressure propaganda, its apoplexy at the centre and apathy at the extremities, can possibly mean, even in an Hegelian sense, an active participation in social initiative which is remotely comparable to that which can be realized where the consumer's bid is the criterion. And I see no aid to the prospects of political democracy (whose problems, heaven knows, are difficult enough without further complication) from the general " politicalization " of decisions regarding private goods.

But what about the choice between present and future? To what extent are we content to base our investment policy on the propensities of the consumers? Note please my terminology. I say " base our policy upon ". I do not say " let it be determined by " ; the imperfections of the capital market as a mechanism for marrying the propensity to consume and the disposition to invest are so notorious that it is especially necessary, in this connection, to make it clear that it is criteria and not the machinery of control which are under discussion. Most of the over-all plans that we know in practice have their main *raison d'être* in an attempt to raise the rate of capital creation above the point which it would have reached, if the investment plan had been based upon the probable volume of voluntary saving in a condition of brisk employment. From the standpoint I have been adopting, what is there to say about such projects?

I am fairly clear that we are here in a region where extreme purism is apt to become somewhat ridiculous. It would be absurd to suggest that in the modern world, with its joint-stock companies undertaking so large a proportion of the aggregate volume of saving, the collective propensity to consume bears any narrow or immediate relation to private propensities — though that may well be an argument for reform of the law relating to the distribution of profits rather than against any attempt to bring total accumulation into relation with the inclinations of the consumers. Moreover, a substantial fraction of the capital accumulation of the present day tends to go to the production of public goods; and it is not usually urged by economists that these should always be financed by borrowing. And finally, if we are very purist in this connection, we must be very careful as to the degree to which in other contexts — before other audiences — we extend *ex cathedra* blessing to the vagaries of gold supply at various periods of history. There can be little doubt that a slightly rising price level, due to suitable monetary policy or fortunate monetary accidents, may quite perceptibly alter the volume of annual accumulation; and I doubt very much whether, taking into account all the manifold complexities of life, we should all want to frown upon this.

But having said this and thus having paid my tribute to fashionable argument, I should like to enter my protest against fashionable exaggerations. It is one thing to admit that there is a good deal that is arbitrary in the collective propensity to consume as registered through current institutions and that some slight gingering-up of capital accumulation by monetary tendencies probably does not do much harm and may do some good. It is quite another thing to argue that it is usually a good thing to force upon the different members of the community, through the apparatus of politics, a rate of accumulation fundamentally out of relation to their true preferences formulated individually. Through the obscure mists of history it is perhaps possible to perceive cases where, *taking everything into account* — including the danger of war,— decisions of this sort may be said to have been justified. Such cases may recur in the future. But I find it difficult to discover, in the principles of the free society, any clear justification for such methods as a general procedure. I am not greatly impressed by appeal to Ramsey's demonstration that we should seek to reach " bliss " at a pace much smarter than our private inclinations make probable; I acknowledge some obligation to posterity but not necessarily all that. And when it is argued that political decisions to go forward with plans of this sort are as democratic as decisions based upon estimates of voluntary savings, I am afraid that I remain very sceptical. It may very well be that if the people are told through the radio that a gigantic development plan is the true road to recovery they will welcome it. But can we be so sure which way their votes would go, if the same thing were put to them in terms of restriction of current consumption. I confess that when I look around and see important communities whose political equilibrium is obviously endangered by lack of consumption goods asked to acquiesce in vast plans which necessarily involve, either import of capital on a scale which is quite improbable or an indefinite prolongation of shortages, I wonder where moderation and good sense have gone. And I find it no consolation at all that, in present conditions, these ill-considered schemes are very likely to break down. General chaos is no cure for collective schizophrenia.

And now I have almost done. My reflections on the functions of demand price as the criterion of future production have led me into very deep waters. I began with a contrast between mechanisms of choice and the logic of their mode of operation. I have been led to the threshold of the great controversies of our day in which two conceptions of the ends of the state are in mortal conflict with each other. At this point I must desist, although I hope I have left you in no doubt where my own sympathies lie. The questions which are involved here are questions which far transcend the scope of economic analysis; they involve indeed the most ultimate questions of all concerning the nature and purpose of society.

But I have one concluding observation. As I have said already, the question which I have been discussing here, the question relating to the criteria of production, is not the same as the question whether production should be organized on a collectivist or an individualist basis: you can conceive a private organization of production which ministered widely to collective demand; you can conceive a collectivist organization of production which was directed to satisfying the demands of private consumers. And, important as is this question of organization, I am inclined to urge that the question I have been discussing is to-day even more important. The questions of ownership and organization are certainly very fundamental; the differences which separate those who believe in over-all collectivism from those who believe in private property and decentralized initiative are serious. But I have the strong conviction that it is the dispute about ends which matters most. If we can agree upon ends, discussion of the question of means can be much calmer and more dispassionate. An individualist who recognizes the importance of public goods and a collectivist who recognizes the desirability of the maximum freedom of individual consumption will find many points of agreement in common. The biggest dividing line of our day is, not between those who differ about organization as such, but between those who differ about the ends which organization has to serve.

That, at least, is my excuse for dwelling at some length on these problems of general objectives before proceeding to the more specifically economic problems of organization and control which will be the subject of the following lectures.

THE RATIONALE OF THE WAR ECONOMY

MY first lecture was devoted chiefly to a discussion of the objectives of economic policy, of the choice of goods to be produced and the mechanism whereby this choice can be ascertained. My lecture to-day will be concerned with a much more concrete survey of certain aspects of the economic system which evolved during the recent hostilities. I proceed this way rather than towards an immediate discussion of peace-time organization, because I believe that the contrast and comparison of the necessities of peace and war brings into sharp relief some of the main problems which contemporary discussion is apt to overlook. I shall try to deal with three problems : why the war controls were necessary, why they worked as well as they did and why they are now very obviously failing to do the job.

1. *Why the War Controls were Necessary*

To go back for a moment to the viewpoint of my last lecture, it should be clear, as I hinted then, that the decision to make war is akin to the decision to furnish any other kind of public service. It is a decision which can only be made by the political organ of state — you cannot conceive a choice of peace or war which was expressed through the market. But in the case of modern wars, which are essentially a struggle for existence, it is a decision which has a peculiar overriding status. He who wills the end wills the means. The nation which decides upon total war must be supposed to decide, whether it realizes it fully or not, upon all the consequential decisions which are necessary to bring the war to a satisfactory conclusion. That is to say, it must be supposed to decide upon a suspense of its capacity to decide upon a host of matters which, in more normal conditions, it is not to be supposed it would surrender at all willingly. No doubt this is a grotesque rationalization of what actually happens in the stress of mass emotion. But it is the only way of making sense, or democratic sense, of what follows.

The die having been cast, however, there remains the question of organization. On what basis is the life of the community to be run while the war is taking place? Are the means of making war to be procured through the mechanism of the free market or is that mechanism to be suspended? Is it to be a matter of business as usual or a matter of war-time collectivism? In the light of recent experience, you may think this question to be frivolous; and, lest your prejudices should be unnecessarily aroused, I will confess to you at once that I propose to answer in favour of war-time collectivism. But if we approach the matter with completely open minds, the answer is not immediately obvious. After all, many public goods are supplied by private enterprise ; why not the public good, success in total war ?

Let me try to state the argument in favour of private enterprise. This will probably irritate you. But if you bear in mind that later on I am going to help you out by developing several, as they seem to me, very powerful arguments against it, you may be able to sit through the ordeal. It is always worth while trying to understand the point of view of the other side — although I fancy that, in this question, there are very few who can be so described nowadays, at least on this side of the Atlantic.

From the economic point of view the making of war is essentially a matter of command over resources. Hence, it is argued, the essential problem is a problem of public finance. If the government is willing to tax sufficiently drastically and to arrange its borrowing on a non-inflationary basis, there need arise no occasion for more direct controls. If the government is willing to take enough purchasing power out of the hands of the citizens, there need be no fear of inflation and no fear that private demand will make hampering claims on factors of production which should be transferred to the public sector. In the private sector, any rise which takes place in the price of consumption goods will reflect a state of real scarcity and will help to choke off demand, so obviating the possibility of queues and shortages. In the war sector, the stimulus of profit, unimpeded by the delays and contradictions almost necessarily inherent in a system oᵢ central control, will result in a response of supply to any extent deemed desirable. On this side, too, the price mechanism can be expected to perform its customary allocatory functions. The alleged necessity for control arises simply from the fear of inflation; if a proper financial policy is pursued this fear is illusory.

Such, in very crude outline, is the case for regarding public finance as the essential instrument of the war economy — the fiscal theory of war control, as it may be called, if we like short labels. And, whatever we may think of its ultimate validity, I think that, if we are to be fair, we must acknowledge that it is a theory with an intellectual basis which is not to be regarded as contemptible; it is not just a collection of prejudices and slogans. We must acknowledge too — what should give us, as economists, some prejudice in its favour — that it is not lacking in courage. It contemplates financial measures more drastic than any government has been willing to attempt in any major war. It is to be most sharply distinguished from the fatuous and easy-going view which urges business as usual and no untoward increases in taxation — the view which has so often been adopted in practice and which has so inevitably led to chaos and inflation. The fiscal theory is not a theory which has been tried and has failed. It is a theory which no government has ever had the will to make the effective basis of policy in a war of any great dimensions.

I am, indeed, prepared to go beyond these tepid acknowledgments and to urge that in a certain range of cases there is real force and validity in this kind of prescription. For the conduct of the small wars of the liberal age in which this theory was current, I have little doubt that it was good advice. When all that was required for the success of operations was some enlargement of a volunteer army, some quickening of munition replacement, the belief that finance was the sinews of war and that a courageous use of the tax instrument was the main desideratum of economic policy was surely thoroughly justified. There was no need to transform the whole basis of production and distribution in order to muster resources for the wars of the mid-nineteenth century. The chief danger there was not that munitions or recruiting would be short but that money would be too plentiful. To insist upon taxation rather than recourse to the printing press was sound practical wisdom.

But when we come to the wars of our own age, with their vast demands on men and materials, their acute scarcities, and their utter domination of the field of business confidence, then, as I see it, the fiscal theory loses its cogency. Indeed, I would say that the attempt to apply it to such a situation is an apt illustration of the dangers, of which Marshall so often warned us, of taking universal methods of analysis to be universal principles of application, of believing that what can be confidently asserted of small changes can be equally confidently asserted of large, and that reactions which may be expected within a given structure of customs and expectations may still be expected to follow if that structure does not exist. I do not say that in conditions of total war a vigorous financial policy is not necessary; I am sure it is. But I do say that there are strong theoretical grounds, in my judgment adequately borne out by practice, for believing that it is not enough. Let me try to demonstrate this in greater detail.

May I begin with a somewhat practical consideration. The advocates of the fiscal theory are apt sometimes to speak as if *any* degree of inflation which occurs during war-time must be attributed entirely to moral cowardice on the part of the governments concerned, and to urge that, in pure theory at least, inflation is something which is wholly avoidable. Hence, it is argued, any controls which depend for their justification upon the presence of inflation are, strictly speaking, unnecessary.

There is something heroic about this position which must surely command our admiration. But I doubt very much whether it is tenable, at any rate, if " pure theory " takes account of time intervals and other intractable data. Of course, if the system is in a severe state of under-employment when war breaks out or when rearmament begins, a good deal of money may be spent without giving rise to any developments which can properly be regarded as inflationary. The under-employment at the outset of the U.S. machine was doubtless responsible for the degree to which it was possible there to increase production without resorting to the severer measures of our over-all regimentation. But, assuming that fairly brisk business prevails, then it seems to me that to believe that you can get through without some initial inflationary expansion is to ignore very obvious facts. It is surely not open to question that, if need arises, money will have to be spent. In war, time is more important than money — it is the one priority which is virtually absolute; and to delay the maximum acceleration of expansion in the war sector for reasons of financial purism would be folly. But it is equally unquestionable too that, whereas increased expenditure must start from the word "go", increased revenue can only come in after an interval. Our theories of public finance are all too apt to ignore the time-lags in tax collection. The gap, therefore, must be filled by increased borrowing; and it is not easy to see how, in practice, some of this borrowing will not be inflationary. It is tempting to conceive a movement of interest rates and an informal rationing of credits which would keep this process in check. But contracts on government account are entitled to unlimited credit. To disentangle the sheep from the goats in this respect in such manner as to apply limits only to demands which had no relation, direct or indirect, to the war sector would be a matter of extreme difficulty. Indeed, its successful performance assumes the existence of just such an apparatus of controls as the fiscal theory assumes to be unnecessary.

In saying this I am anxious not to be misunderstood. I am not seeking to provide any justification for departure from the most rigorous financial precepts. Nor do I wish to question the considerable public service which the advocates of this theory may render incidentally by insisting, in season and out of season, on the necessity for financing the war by non-inflationary measures. But I confess to a sneaking conviction that the zealots of this theory import an atmosphere of extreme unreality into the discussion, if they argue as if, in practice, no inflation need take place and that hence there is no need for the other measures which the threat of inflation may make necessary. Quite apart from the obvious political diffi- culties in bringing ministers and popular assemblies to an immediate realization of the need for the most drastic financial measures, I am inclined to believe that the technical reasons I have adduced make it extremely im- probable that some degree of inflation can be avoided.

Nevertheless, I should be extremely sorry to rest the case against the sufficiency of the fiscal theory upon grounds of the inevitability of inflation. After all, the degree of inflation which is unavoidable is strictly limited. If that were all that were involved, there would be a strong case for letting prices rise to the level of the limited ex- pansion and then proceeding on the basis of the price system and free enterprise. I am convinced, however, that there are deeper analytical reasons why, where total war is involved, this argument rests upon misapprehension. It is to these matters that I now wish to direct your attention.

Consider first the manning of the armed forces. It has been the tradition of this country to recruit its peace-time forces on a voluntary basis, with rates of pay and other attractions so adjusted in relation to the prevailing wage level as to secure the numbers deemed desirable; and in the smaller wars of a less brutal age this system still persisted. Yet, on the two recent occasions when we have been fighting for our existence, it has had to be abandoned in favour of conscription. I wonder whether, at this time of day, there is anyone who would seriously argue that it would have been wise to rely on voluntary recruitment. It is quite true, as I expect many of you who have been conscripted are thinking, that the market system was not put to a very severe test. Rates of pay were not raised so as greatly to increase the differential attraction of service. Doubtless, if they had been raised enough, many more would have been tempted in. But would it have been prudent to rely upon this incentive? Might there not have been so many people whose voluntary supply price in this line of production was virtually infinite, that essential requirements were left unfulfilled? There is, I think, a very solid utilitarian justification for the popular view that, when the safety of the state is seriously threatened, the obligation to pay taxes in money becomes supplemented by the obligation, so to speak, to pay taxes in kind, to render dues not only in money but in the services of whatever factors happen to be at one's disposal.

It is not only in the armed forces that the supply of labour needs to be assured. It is necessary also that there should be adequate man-power for munition-making and other essential services. Here, too, in conditions of total war, to rely only on the market mechanism is to leave too much to the play of individual idiosyncrasy. In the recent war, although in this sphere the approach to compulsion at first was much more tentative and indirect than in the sphere of military service, we eventually reached a state of affairs in which virtually the whole adult population under the pension age was subject to powers of direction. It is true that the analogy with conscription must not be pushed too far. More recourse was had to the stimulus of differential rates of pay; in a just view of the history of the war due tribute should be paid to the part played by voluntary movement in the initial process of reshuffling. Moreover, when the shift had taken place, rates of pay were never on the army basis; this, not only because of the possibility of trade union resistance but because, the utmost output per head being essential, it was necessary for there to be full opportunity for increased earnings, both by way of piece rates and by way of overtime payments. But when all account has been taken of the scope left to the cash incentive, the fact remains that the market proved inadequate and that it was found necessary to supplement its action by a strong framework of compulsion. It was found necessary, too, to limit the production of non-essential private goods lest any labour not subject to immediate compulsion should be tempted to linger there rather than turn to work on more essential business.

Similar considerations apply to the use of material resources. Reliance upon a voluntary response to a financial incentive is reasonable enough when the response needed is small in relation to the total national resources. But when it is essential that the response shall be total —

that no resources which could be useful remain unused — or put to uses that are not essential — it is not enough. Powers must be taken to commandeer and direct the use of stocks, plants, land and means of transport, and, if necessary, to prohibit their use for other purposes. Nothing must be withheld. In total war, the agreeable liberty not to take the price offered if one prefers otherwise, must necessarily be in suspense.

There is another aspect of this matter which I think deserves separate attention. To be reasonably certain of a sufficient and swift response to a change in the conditions of demand, it is necessary for the entrepreneurs to be reasonably certain that the change is not suddenly to be reversed before they have had a chance to amortize the capital investment. Now in war-time this degree of certainty is not present. The risk factor which the entrepreneur has to take account of is altogether abnormal. The duration of war is unknown. The danger of enemy action by land and sea may be very great. In such circumstances, the immediate financial incentive would have to be inordinately great if unguaranteed private enterprise were to be induced to take the risks of erecting special installations in vulnerable places, of importing over perilous seas, of locking up capital in undertakings the demand for whose products must collapse on the unknown date when hostilities come to an end. If it is necessary to the state to be assured that these things will be done, the state must bear at least part of the risk. It must be prepared to give special guarantees, to underwrite special undertakings and even itself to go into business on a very large scale.

So much for the conditions of supply. But what about the mechanism for the allocation of resources? Here, too, conditions are completely different from anything which is assumed in the peace-time models. The theory of the normal market as a means of allocating the factors of production rests essentially on the assumption of limited power to demand. If the system is in a state of fairly full utilization and if there is some over-all check on monetary expansion, then the extent to which any particular price can be bid up is limited. The various concerns, with their limited finances, bid against one another. As the prices rise, some demands are choked off until the available supplies are parcelled out according to the demands which still remain active. There are all sorts of comments and criticisms which can be made upon the working of this process. But it would be silly to deny that, in a rough and ready way, it can be made to perform what is expected of it.

In war-time, however, it is different. The competitors in the market, or some of them at any rate, are working to government orders. So far as they are concerned, credit is virtually unlimited. Many of them will be working on a cost plus profit basis — this not because the authorities are ignorant of the palpable objections to this method, but because, at the outset at least, there is no time to fix up anything else. Even where this is not the case, there is no practical limitation on what they may spend in order to get the necessary resources. There is, therefore, virtually no limit on the possible upward movement of prices. There are present all the theoretical conditions necessary for a cumulative Wicksellian process. To argue that this can be defeated by appropriate movements of the interest rate does not seem to me a very helpful or practical suggestion. It would be interesting to see the rate of interest which would secure a proper allocation of alloy steel between Admiralty and Ministry of Supply contractors.

In such circumstances recourse is had to price fixing. But if the mechanism of the market is thus paralysed, it is necessary to provide other means for the performance of its functions. On the demand side, quantitative allocation is necessary; on the supply side, a machinery of control which brings it about that the diminution of prospective profits in one line does not lead to diversion of resources to others.

For somewhat different reasons you get a similar suspension of the market mechanism in regard to the supply of final products, not merely in the war sector, but also in what is left of the sector for the supply of private goods. As I argued in my first lecture, the development of severe shortages in the supply of essential consumption goods tends to bring about a situation in which, under uncontrolled prices, the pressure on the real incomes of the poorest consumers is felt to be intolerable; and since, in such circumstances, supply is likely to be inelastic, the windfall profits which result will be the object of particular resentment. It is perhaps conceivable that such a situation could be dealt with by taxation and by measures of forced saving which would reduce expenditure to a level of virtual equality. In practice, however, this is a vain hope. It is not merely reluctance to tax, it is also fear of the effects on incentive, which really puts this alternative out of court. In its absence, there is nothing for it but recourse to price fixing and rationing and the further measures of control of supply which such policies make inevitable.

For all these reasons, the necessities of supply, the abnormal conditions of risk, the unreliability of market price as an allocation mechanism when government credit is unlimited, and the development of severe shortage on the consumption front, it is surely clear that in a major war the fiscal theory of war economy must break down. And if it breaks down anywhere, it is likely very shortly to break down everywhere. It is true that not all the embarrassments and difficulties which I have indicated are likely to be immediately apparent. The development of severe shortage takes time ; some parts of the economy are much more vulnerable than others. But there is a sort of snowball logic about this kind of intervention. You intervene here to fix prices, or to sustain supply, and automatically you are drawn on to prevent developments elsewhere from frustrating your original intention. Once you are committed anywhere to this kind of policy on a large scale, it is almost inevitable that you will find yourself committed nearly everywhere else. This is not an argument for a pedantic multiplication of controls for the sake of control. But it is an argument for recognizing the inherent necessities of total war and, if the necessary mechanism is not planned already, losing no time in making your preparations. In such conditions there can be nothing more dangerous than delaying action in the hope that some fluke of circumstance will make it unnecessary to grasp the nettle. It is perhaps a legitimate source of satisfaction that, in this country with its traditions of a free economy, this was sooner perceived and more effectively acted upon than in enemy countries where authoritarian ideologies had so muddled the heads of those in control that they no longer realized the necessities of the system which they were trying to operate.

2. *The Effectiveness of Control in War-time*

This brings me to my second main problem. The reasons I have given may be quite sufficient to explain why private enterprise and the market were inadequate. But they do not explain at all why the controls which were put in their place succeeded as well as they did. And this is a real problem. You have to be very naïve indeed to believe that to suspend the market and to take extraordinary powers of control, in itself, makes things very easy. The general presumption indeed is the other way. Central control is really not at all easy. The incentive of private gain, however poorly you may think of it from the ethical point of view, does provide some stimulus to effort and economy. If it is removed or partially suspended and replaced by orders from the centre, there is no certainty in the nature of things that the machine will continue to work smoothly. There is no certainty that the orders will be obeyed. There is no certainty that, in the absence of orders from the centre, people will continue to act in a more or less useful manner.

But supposing this difficulty is surmounted, there still remains the general problem of planning. The market, with all its imperfections, does provide some basis of economic calculation, some more or less automatic basis of allocation. If it is suspended, if the prices which persist are no longer the resultant of the various forces of supply and demand, on what basis are you to plan? Here are your various resources, your labour force, your stocks and your material equipment, many of which, having regard to the exigencies of war, are obviously out of place in their peace-time uses. What computations of the gain and loss of various possible shifts are feasible without a price system? As you know, the problem of calculation in a collectivist community was the subject of extensive debate in the years before the war. Some of us urged that it would be difficult, and some that it would be easy, to establish a system of market prices on the basis of which such a society could plan. But most of us agreed that, in the absence of prices of some sort, a rational disposition of resources would usually be extremely difficult: and, so far as I can see, nothing that happened during the war did anything to shake that general presumption.

How then did it come about that, having substituted control from the centre for dispersed initiative and suspended the mechanism which makes normal economic calculation possible, we managed to struggle through?

In attempting to answer this question I do not think we shall get the picture into proper perspective if we do not recognize the part played by the sense of social obligation and unity of purpose which our peculiar perils invoked. This is not a matter which has much analytical interest; there is not much to say about it for textbook purposes. But you will find many things very hard to explain if you leave it out of account. Let me take one small instance from a vast field of possible examples — the comparative success of the price-fixing regulations. Anyone who knows the machinery which was supposed to work these regulations must admit that it would have been completely inadequate for its purpose if there had not existed a strong disposition to co-operate on the part of traders and merchants. You used to read from time to time of the activities of the local price committees and occasional prosecutions in the courts. But you will get things completely out of perspective if you believe that it was this apparatus of coercion which was responsible for the comparative infrequency of black-market activities. It was the will to co-operate and the sense of responsibility of the majority of those to whom these regulations applied. Had there been no such will, no such sense of responsibility, the regulations would have broken down over a large field, as they are clearly beginning to break down at the present day. This is but one example of the general atmosphere which made so many difficult things easy. In the absence of such a spirit of spontaneous solidarity only the forcible liquidation of all opponents of the regime could have made possible so high a degree of mobilization.

Of course this is only part of the story. If spontaneous zeal and co-operativeness were one side of the shield, universal powers of direction were the other. I have mentioned the disposition of the people first, because I am fully convinced that in the absence of this disposition the apparatus of coercion would have jammed. But the apparatus was there none the less, and if you wish to understand why the materials and the labour were, roughly speaking, to be found where it was intended that they should be, you must take into account, not only the unique disposition of the people but also the all-embracing powers of control and direction on the part of the government. At the peak of war mobilization only the old and women with young children could take jobs or leave jobs without the permission of the Ministry of Labour and National Service, and the producer who was not under orders, direct or indirect, was the rarest of rare exceptions.

All this is fairly obvious although, perhaps, now that many of these powers have lapsed, it is apt to be forgotten. What is not so obvious, but what I am convinced is absolutely fundamental to a proper understanding of what happened, was the immense simplification of the general planning problem which arose from the peculiar nature of the war emergency. You all know that in general equilibrium analysis there occur certain limiting cases — *e.g.* when all supply curves are parallel to the x axis — when an otherwise intolerably complex problem suddenly becomes capable of being understood in terms of comparatively simple formulae. I am inclined to argue that, in the first approximation at least, the planning problem in total war presents a somewhat analogous case. Let me try to explain what I mean.

In total war there is only one prime object of policy, the achievement of total victory. To that object all other aims are subordinate, by that criterion all special operations must be judged. Whatever may be the outcome of victory, whether it be a positive gain or a position perceptibly worse than that from which you started, if the alternative is annihilation, then, while the will to survive persists at all, no sacrifice seems too great. What is to come after does not matter; if there is no victory there is no future. The nice calculations of the advantages and disadvantages of alternative compromise positions, characteristic of the wars of other times, are inappropriate here. Total war is a matter of death or victory. It is the nature of the case that there is no intermediate position.

In such circumstances the major problem of allocation, the allocation of resources between private and public consumption, undergoes a most drastic simplification. For the time being private consumption, which normally is an end in itself, becomes something which is purely instrumental. Attention to private welfare is certainly an

47

important matter: up to a certain point, indeed, it has an almost absolute priority over almost everything else. But it is important merely, so to speak, for operational reasons. If the people are not in good health and good heart, the conduct of the war may be endangered. But beyond that point, in this calculus of hell-fire and desperation, the value of additional private welfare is zero; direct operations claim everything. Thanks to the totalitarians, it is in the service of this hideous logic that we have had to spend the best years of our lives.

Hence the division between the private and the public sectors becomes, as it were, a merely technical business. You have to ask what is the minimum which will keep the people alive and fighting fit — and having made sure that enough resources in the shape of shipping, stocks and man-power are devoted to this end, you can push everything else into the war sector. No doubt this way of putting things conceals many difficulties. The determination of the minima necessary to maintain health and morale is by no means an easy matter; the doctors do not always agree on what is necessary for health; the politicians debate endlessly how much austerity is tolerable. But the fact remains that, if you can treat consumption as something to be determined by reference to this kind of criterion and ignore all other considerations, the simplification of the allocation problem is so great as to be virtually a change in its nature.

So far as the public sector is concerned, the position is somewhat different. Here the problem of action is still essentially a problem of choice between alternatives — political economy and military strategy are both branches of the general theory of rational action. The solution of these problems involves complicated weighing of the military effectiveness of different uses of resources, attack from the Channel Ports or from Mediterranean bases, the enlargement of the army or the production of bombing aircraft. No one who has assisted in any way in the business of strategic planning will wish to minimize the difficulty or the complexity of the choices which have to be made. Nevertheless the number of alternative broad strategic plans which promise hope of military success is severely limited; and, once the decisions are taken on this plane, much of the detail is consequential. The day-to-day problems of allocating scarce labour, scarce materials, scarce capacity, scarce shipping between the different claimant departments were very formidable. But in the last resort they were matters for the Defence Committee; it was the big strategic decisions which really governed everything else. No doubt, in decisions of this sort, the absence of an over-all yardstick, capable of reducing to a common denominator the relative gain and cost of alternative operations, must be a profound limitation on the possibility of rational action. If a military intuition goes wrong, its consequences may be catastrophic, in a sense which is seldom to be expected of any decision which can be governed by cash computations. But the fact remains that the narrowness of the ultimate objective, the defeat of the enemy, gives a certain unity to the framework of planning which at least makes possible some sort of direct decision which is not wholly arbitrary. It was for that reason, I am convinced, that despite the suspension of the ordinary apparatus of calculation and the absence of any objective value denominator of the ultimate physical resources, our machinery of control did not lack a certain minimum of coherency and force.

We must not exaggerate the degree of efficiency of our war-time arrangements and improvisations. The degree of waste and misdirection was doubtless such that if any but the highest stakes of all had been at issue, this kind of cost alone would have been judged to be prohibitive. But the end was not wholly an accident. " The reason you won and we lost ", the wretched Speer is reported to have said, " was that you made total war and we did not."

3. *The Difficulties of Control when War is Over*

But now the war is over and we are confronted with new problems and animated by different aspirations ; and, in this position, it is obvious that the machinery of control, or what is left of it, is not working particularly well. Is this a matter of accident — a matter of personal deficiency or political mismanagement ? Or is there some more fundamental change which brings it about that the machine is now less adequate to its task ? This, you may remember, was the third general problem which I promised to tackle in this lecture.

The Rationale of the War Economy

Now I have no doubt that you suspect, and I have no concern to deny, that I have no particular love for war-time controls as normal institutions for a society at peace. I shall be talking more about this problem in my next lecture. But I should like to make it clear, here and now, that I am by no means of the view that, in our present state of acute disequilibrium, the immediate abandonment of the control system is advisable. On the contrary, I am against it. But while I do not wish to see the mechanism precipitately dismantled, I do think that the troubles from which we are now suffering offer a very vivid illustration of the difficulties inherent in its use when it is put to tackle peace-time problems. It will clear the way for more positive proposals next time if I proceed to develop this a little further.

The first thing to realize is that the allocation problem has once again completely changed its nature. You can no longer express the object of economic policy in terms of a single concrete objective. Gone is the yardstick of military effectiveness. Gone is the willingness of the citizens to be clamped down to a minimum standard of consumption. Housing, capital re-equipment, the needs of the balance of payments, the insistent demand of the consumer for something more on which to spend his money, all in their manifold complexity of detail jostle shoulders, so to speak, struggling for higher allocations of resources. Of course, if it gives you any satisfaction, you can still provide a formal description of the ultimate goal which has a unitary appearance. Nobody is likely to quarrel with the statement that the object of policy should be to maximize welfare over time. But this is to state the problem, not to solve it. In the absence of a measuring rod, however conventional, the problem of maximization remains unresolved.

Consider, for instance, the allocation of timber. Heaven knows that, during the war, this problem was sufficiently difficult. Hutments, boxing, sleepers, pit-props, aeroplanes, vehicles — there was a vast list of possible users which had to have their claims examined and pruned so as to fit the available supplies. But in the last analysis the criteria were comparatively simple. First of all, you had to ask of any claim of the civil departments, " Is this absolutely necessary for maintaining minimum standards ? " If not, it could be cut out. Then, if it were a claim for a war use or for an essential service, you had to ask, " How important is the marginal application here compared to marginal applications elsewhere ? " ; and although that was very hard to decide in detailed cases, you always had your general strategic plan as an ultimate court of reference. But now you have no such simple criterion by which to judge applications. Timber is needed for export, both for manufacture and consignment ; the opportunities of selling different quantities at different prices in different markets are almost infinitely various. Timber is needed for housing and construction : there is no easy method of deciding between the claims of dwelling-houses, schools, hospitals, factory construction and so on. Over a vast field of manufacture for the home market, timber is in urgent demand. By what yardstick are marginal products to be compared in all these multitudinous uses? Of course, the process of allocation continues; it is not true to say that there are no plans. The King's business must be carried on. But who among us would be willing to assert with any degree of confidence that one pattern rather than another is most likely to maximize welfare?

This is only one example of the increased difficulties which develop everywhere, as soon as the peculiar simplifications arising from concentration on a single strategic plan have ceased to be possible. And, in many ways, the example I have given underestimates the difficulties. For, after all, timber is not an ultimate factor of production. At a pinch we could have relatively more timber if we were willing to pay even higher prices and sacrifice even more foreign exchange, that is to say, sacrifice other essential imports. We could have more foreign exchange if we were willing to sacrifice more domestic consumption or more capital re-equipment. Until there is some common denominator to which you can reduce, if not all, at least most, of the multitudinous alternative uses of your heterogeneous resources, all particular production plans are necessarily shots in the dark. It is clear that some are likely to be more sensible than others. But the extent to which you can hope to plan without the possibility of really bad mistakes is limited.

I am afraid there is no way out of these difficulties by the frequent reiteration of the magic formula, social priorities. The authors of this incantation have had a grand run for their money in the popular press and elsewhere. But if we wish words to communicate thought rather than to create a comfortable state of mind, I must say that they are singularly unhelpful. For the word priority, in its technical connotation, stands for an administrative device which is just the reverse of what is wanted at the present moment. To grant priority to any particular product is to rule that, for the time being, any manufacture of that product has a prior right over all others for the necessary services and materials. But although, in a severe emergency, it may be useful to resort to this expedient, as a general method of regulating economic life it spells chaos and confusion. An economic disposition of resources cannot possibly be achieved, if you decree that all resources of a certain kind are to go to one use, none to any of the others — all your alloy steel to tanks, none to battleships and various kinds of engines. The economic problem is essentially a problem of regulating the quantities which go to different uses and securing some rough equality of yield at the margin. It is a problem not of priority but of allocation. If, therefore, the demand for action on a basis of social priorities is taken in a technical sense, it is positively misleading. If, however, it is merely to be regarded as a metaphorical way of speaking, it is simply a re-statement of the problem. We need an allocation of resources which will satisfy the various objectives we have in mind. But we have no objective measure either of the conflicting ends or the effectiveness of the alternative means; and neither the public nor the ministers find it easy to agree on arbitrary rulings. And the more democratic you try to be, the more difficult the task becomes.

Hence demands for strong men, planning committees, new organs of government and so on and so forth.

But even if we had a rigid over-all quantitative five-year plan of the kind which it is so fashionable to demand, and even if the nature of this plan were not such as to defeat one of the main requirements of the present situation, which is maximum decentralization and flexibility, we should still be in difficulties on account of the lack of sanctions to enforce it. I alluded last time to our paradoxical position as regards the cash incentive. I have hinted to-day at the passing of that sense of unity and obligation which, in the absence of cash incentive and compulsion, still gave impetus and momentum to much of the working of the war economy. My survey would not be complete, however, if I did not direct your attention to the almost total disappearance of those powers of control which are almost essential to the smooth running of an economy controlled from the centre, namely, the powers of control over labour. It is quite true that there remain many powers of control by way of licence and allocation. We must not under-estimate the extent to which the material factors of production are still dependent on orders from the centre. But the power to direct labour to the jobs in which it is wanted, the power to prevent labour from leaving jobs which are regarded as essential, have gone; and so far as I can see, it would be most imprudent to base our plans and our recommendations upon the belief that any speedy or complete restoration is possible. In the days when it was my duty to sit through committees which were surveying the prospects of reconversion, nothing impressed me more than the unanimity with which all concerned assumed it as an axiom that the retention of the labour controls was impossible. No one wished to abolish the controls immediately. Many were convinced that some sort of control was inevitable as a permanent arrangement. But one and all assumed that, whatever might be the ideal arrangement, in practice the labour controls must go. And that, of course, is just what has happened. Over a wide field there are no means of compulsion available for ensuring that the right number of men are in the right jobs. However much you may deplore this state of affairs, it is not likely to change greatly unless there is grave deterioration in the general situation.

Thus at a moment when with one part of our minds we crave the comfort and the assurance of an over-all totalitarian plan, with the other part we are unable to take the decisions necessary to bring it into being and unwilling to submit to the measures necessary to carry it out.

In my concluding lecture I shall begin by discussing some possible ways out of the impasse.

THE CONTROL OF PRODUCTION
IN PEACE-TIME

AT the end of my last lecture I had led you to the brink
of a slough of despond. I had shown you an allocation
machinery which was palpably insufficient for the tasks
which were being thrust upon it, and an apparatus of
control and incentive in a state of visible disintegration
I want to begin to-day by pointing to what seems to me
a way whereby, from this dismal position, we might hope
to reach firm ground again ; I shall proceed from this to
a broader view of over-all planning ; and I shall conclude
with a few general observations on the issue of public
versus private ownership of the means of production.
Since my statements are bound to be short, it follows,
from a well-known Marshallian rule (which I acknowledge to be true), that they will almost certainly be partially
wrong. I can only ask for charitable interpretation of the
overtones.

1. *The Problem of the Transition*

To begin, then, with the problem of the transition. In
the first part of my last lecture, you will remember, I set

forth in some detail the main reasons why, when war came, economic controls were necessary : the desirability of complete mobilization, the abnormal risk factor, the unlimited power to demand of contractors on government account, the necessity of sustaining supply in conditions when prices were fixed below the point of market equilibrium. Now if we look at the situation to-day we can see that some at least of these considerations are no longer so compelling as they were. It is clear beyond doubt that we no longer believe in the desirability of over-all compulsion. Conscription, it is true, remains in a very attenuated form. But, as I was emphasizing last time, the labour controls have disappeared; any attempt to reintroduce them would be very strongly resisted. The abnormal risk factor has disappeared. It is true that the future is very uncertain ; political complications may well make entrepreneurs uneasy. But there is no reason to believe that, politics apart, where demand is likely to be sustained, there will be any undue holding back on the part of enterprise : and the uncertainties which are due to politics are clearly within our power to remove. And if there still persists a danger of government contractors bidding against one another with unlimited credit, this is surely something which should be stopped. Difficult as our position is, we are no longer in an emergency in which money is no consideration. There are factors in the external position which to some extent cut across this picture. But, if they were the only complications, I have little doubt that they could be satisfactorily handled by mechanisms which were not generally constrictive.

What remains, however, and what is an intolerable embarrassment to the whole business of reconversion, is the threat of inflation. By this I do not mean that there is a danger, the day after to-morrow, of a run-away rise of prices in the grand European manner: the control mechanism looks after that. I do mean, however, that there is a tendency for expenditure to run ahead of production in such a way that, *if the control mechanism were not there*, commodity prices (and incomes) might get out of hand. This arises in two different ways which although they may be subsumed under a common formula, are, I think, best treated as if they were distinct. On the one hand, our investment plans seem to be in excess of the volume of saving which is likely to accrue at the present level of income. The exact figures in Mr. Paish's estimates of the reconstruction budget [1] for the next ten years may be open to question. But I do not see how we can get away from his general conclusion, that we are planning to invest far more than we should be likely to save at present levels of income without compulsory limitation of consumption. On the other hand, there are the accumulated cash balances and easily realizable investments of the war years, which lurk in the background, so to speak, waiting to rush out into consumption whenever a favourable opportunity presents itself — a perpetual distorting influence, if you like to put it that way, of the general

[1] "The Finance of Reconstruction", by F. W. Paish. *London and Cambridge Economic Service Bulletin*, February 1947.

propensity to consume. For both these reasons, while present conditions persist, the continuation of controls is our only safeguard against an inflationary break.

The effects of this state of suppressed inflation are, however, most embarrassing. On the demand side, there is no limitation of the use of resources, save through a machinery of licensing and allocation which, for reasons which I explained last time, is palpably losing grip of the situation. Prices are below the levels at which demand is equal to supply. Hence with large unsatisfied demands almost everywhere, apart from the inadequate and lamed controls, there is no particular reason why resources should go in one direction rather than another. There is a sense of drift and misdirection. The labour force is indeed fully employed. But there is no guarantee that what is produced anywhere at the margin has more significance in any sense than what could otherwise be produced; a high level of employment is important but it is not enough. Stocks tend to run down without any prospect of replacement. New bottlenecks appear without any guarantee of the operation of forces tending to their elimination. At the same time, on the supply side the incentive has gone out of the system. What is the use of increased pay if it carries with it no certain prospect of increased real income? We are suffering, on a small scale, from the disease which is showing itself in much greater proportions elsewhere. If anyone doubts the disintegrating effects of suppressed inflation, let him look at the present state of Germany, where he will see our present symptoms magnified a hundredfold like great warning shadows on the wall.

If, therefore, we do not wish to retreat to a system of economic totalitarianism which, I am convinced, would be quite incompatible with our present conceptions of democracy, the first requirement of policy is that we should get this dropsy out of our system. This is not a policy of deflation. Despite the Chancellor of the Exchequer, who denounces his friendly advisers for suggesting what he proceeds to *pretend* to do, to remove inflationary tendencies is not to resort to deflation, *i.e.* to a contraction of money incomes. We need a policy which will avoid both inflation and deflation of incomes and which will keep planned saving and planned investment in a proper relation of equality.

How is this to be done? Contrary, perhaps, to your expectations, I am not prepared here and now to recommend a rise in interest rates. I say this, not because I believe that the interest structure, properly manipulated, cannot be a most potent instrument for regulating the rate of investment and for allocating supplies of capital, but because I fear the effect on the budget of a rise which, in present circumstances, would be sufficiently great to be effective. I am not sure about this. I can easily imagine circumstances in which a rise in interest rates might be the least of many alternative evils; I have no sympathy with the fashion which would have us believe that interest rates have no selective influence on investment. But, at the moment, until other measures have been tried and failed I am not in favour of such a policy; though I would like to observe *en passant* that I do not think the situation has been made any easier by the policy of trying to force the rate of interest down — a policy which, I am clear, does not flow from Keynesian prescriptions.

But if, for reasons of public finance, the rate of interest is at present ruled out, what remains? In recent months, Mr. Hawtrey has been recommending a surgical operation, in the Belgian manner, whereby a proportion of outstanding currency and credit would be sterilized. This could undoubtedly be effective, though the administrative complications are formidable. But it is extremely drastic treatment and although, if the situation deteriorates, we may eventually have to do something of the sort, I do not favour it here and now; I doubt if the situation demands it. In my judgment, in present circumstances, we could probably get through with something easier. On the one hand, we must prune the programme in the public sector. On the other hand, we should budget for a real surplus. This should be sufficient to close the so-called prospective gap; and if at the same time it were done by means of tax measures which were coupled with the promise of later reduction, *e.g.* a higher purchase tax coming down as the situation improves, we should have a good chance, I fancy, of keeping money from trying to rush out of the hoards.

In such circumstances, I believe, it would be safe to begin to make more use of the price system. Please notice the caution of my formulation. I make no recommendation of an immediate abandonment of all controls. As

I have emphasized before, I do not believe such a step to be desirable. I see little good in letting prices rocket up to a precarious short-period equilibrium, if there is any reason to suppose that in a somewhat longer period they would be at a materially lower level. My conception rather is to ease the strain by letting prices rise by stages, in the hope that as, in this way, the system becomes better organized and less obviously wasteful, production may so expand that a point is reached when most of this machinery becomes unnecessary. I do not want to abolish this kind of control immediately. But I think it would be prudent to work towards its abolition.

At this point may I forestall a possible criticism. Some of you may feel that a policy of this sort is unacceptable because it involves some rise of prices. You would perhaps not mind some restoration of the price system, if it could take place at the present level. But anything above that, you may feel, would involve hardships which would be intolerable to poor consumers.

Now I do not altogether accept the quantitative basis of this attitude. The stabilization policy was introduced when wage rates were about 20 per cent and the cost of living 30 per cent above the pre-war level. The rise in wage rates is now 65 per cent above pre-war, while the cost of living has remained where it was when the policy was started. In a community in which about as much is spent on beer alone as on rent and rates and water charges, it is hard to argue that any rise anywhere in the price of necessities is really an intolerable matter.

But suppose, for the sake of argument, that this were not the case. Suppose that there were solid grounds for fearing that increases of prices would seriously affect the standard of living of important classes of the community. Even so I would argue, as I argued in my first lecture, that that is no argument for perpetuating a state of affairs involving permanent disequilibrium and the inconveniences and injustices of queues and rationing. It is an argument rather for giving these people more money. So that, if I feared hardship from the price changes I regard as desirable, or if — what is really a much more practical issue — there were reason to fear repercussions on the wage level, I would react, not by changing my recommendation regarding prices, but by urging also some increase in income from civil rights for specially affected classes. If, for instance, a diminution in the food subsidies would have these repercussions, it would cost far less to give the 5s. allowance to the first child and perhaps to make some upward adjustment for children beyond the third, than to keep prices where they are and continue subsidies on this scale to everyone.

Before leaving these transitional problems, I think perhaps I ought to say explicitly that while I see no reason against proceeding internally at a fairly smart pace in the direction I have indicated, I see much greater difficulty in moving towards a rapid approach to decontrol in the external sector. I regret this; for there is no doubt that the sort of controls which we are obliged to use in this sector are a great embarrassment to trade in general and a continual temptation to resort to other totalitarian measures. A considerable experience of economic diplomacy during the war has not led me in any way to modify my conviction that economic nationalism is one of the main causes of international friction. But the degree of our external disequilibrium is so great and the uncertainty and disorganization of the world is so extensive that I see no immediate prospect of the abandonment of control of imports. If, in the long run, we are still unable to balance our international accounts without quantitative regulation, there would be a strong argument for altering the rate of exchange; the extent to which we are in the habit of discussing international equilibrium nowadays without mentioning the rate of exchange is a disgrace to economic thinking. But I see no point in juggling about with the rate of exchange until we have much greater certainty, not only with regard to our own position, but also regarding the position of many countries with which we have to trade. And without a nearer approach to equilibrium in our trade balance it would be obvious folly to use up our precious foreign exchange by permitting unlimited import.

Nevertheless, even here I think we could make the task easier if we were more prepared to use devices which had more in them of the automatisms of a market system. So far as imports are concerned, I do not think we can yet forgo the use of quota restrictions. But what is the objection to working towards auctioning what quotas we allow? Similarly, so far as exports are concerned, I do not doubt the desirability of the various measures of exhortation and surreptitious pressure which are at present the main sanctions of the export drive. But I doubt very much whether they are sufficient or whether the system as such is permanently viable. To get the volume of exports which is necessary we need a strong continuing incentive in the shape of an appropriate relationship of prices and costs. And I see no reason why, as soon as the war was over, we should not have increased the incentive to export by a sharp increase in the purchase tax. I should indeed be prepared to argue that our failure to have more extensive recourse to this instrument was one of the principal mistakes of our present financial policy. From the point of view of the needs of the transition, you can hardly go wrong with the purchase tax. It mops up purchasing power; if reductions later are promised, it keeps cash balances inactive; and it creates an automatic stimulus to export which, to put it mildly, is a valuable adjunct to any forms of direct control which are found to be practically effective.

All this, however, is in the nature of a digression. The main point that I am trying to make in connection with the problem of transition is that, before we can hope to do anything else effectively, we must try to get rid of inflation. Whatever we may think about the difficulties of dispensing with the physical controls, within a system which is in financial equilibrium, we can surely agree that such difficulties are likely to be multiplied a hundredfold within a system which is not.

2. *General Financial Planning*

This brings me back to the problems of policy which may be expected to persist, even when the problems of the transition are over. And here I should like to say at once that I do not think that the problem of securing over-all financial equilibrium is one which we are ever likely to be able to think out of the picture. Whatever we may think of the virtues of the price system as a mechanism of allocation, whatever views we may hold of the alleged automatism of the price and private enterprise system as regards *relative* demand and *relative* supply, I am quite clear that as an instrument for maintaining reasonable constancy of *aggregate* demand it has most profound limitations. Perhaps even here it is possible to exaggerate; there are influences in such a system, at any rate as we have known it in the past, which prevent it from being wholly unstable; it is not treating the subject with the seriousness which it deserves to regard the comparative stability of the pre-1914 system as being entirely a matter of accident. Nevertheless, the limits within which instability is possible may very easily become inconveniently wide; and I am fully persuaded that it is a permanent function of policy to devise measures and institutions for narrowing them. I confess that I have not always held this conviction as strongly as I do to-day. Indeed, looking back, I think this is the point on which I am most conscious of a change of point of view, not, I think, due to the war, but rather to the cumulative effect of reflections on pre-war controversies tested in relation to a somewhat new quantitative perspective. I grew up in a tradition in which, while recognition was indeed given to the problems created by the ups and downs of the trade cycle and the fluctuations of aggregate demand, there was a tendency to ignore certain deep-seated possibilities of disharmony, in a way which, I now think, led sometimes to superficiality and sometimes to positive error. I owe much to Cambridge economists, particularly to Lord Keynes and Professor Robertson, for having awakened me from dogmatic slumbers in this very important respect.

Hence, for the avoidance of both inflation and deflation, I favour something which, if you like, you can call over-all financial planning. At the beginning of each appropriate period the government should make estimates both of the amount of expenditure (consumption plus investment) which is needed to maintain aggregate demand on a more or less even keel and of the amount of expenditure which is likely to be forthcoming. Then if there is a discrepancy between the two, either by way of a tendency to a rise or a fall in aggregate expenditure, it should seek, by what measures seem appropriate in that particular situation, to cause it to disappear. In the sector of public investment (which is likely henceforward to be large) it will have to plan in the current sense of the term, as must any entrepreneur charged with the outlay of money. The sector of public consumption (roughly the expenditure side of the budget) is likewise susceptible to direct control. At the same time in the private sectors, both of investment and consumption, there are available a considerable number of indirect controls, chiefly of a fiscal nature, which can be used, at discretion, to supplement these more direct measures. I am not quite sure whether a policy of this sort, which is designed to maintain over-all stability of aggregate demand, while leaving the maximum flexibility between the various constituent items, is correctly to be described by the term planning; for, in current usage, that term has become more and more associated with other meanings. But on the assumption that the real meaning of the word to plan is to attempt to act with foresight and intelligence, I see no reason to refrain from staking a claim to its use. Why on earth should we refrain from designating as planning policies which are likely to be effective and coherent while retaining it for policies which are not likely to have these qualities? At all events, I am convinced that, whatever else is done, a policy of this sort is incumbent on government. It is with great regret that I observe that the excellent custom of combining with the annual budget a survey of the general financial prospects in this respect, which was inaugurated by Sir Kingsley Wood and continued by Sir John Anderson, has been discontinued by the present Chancellor, and that, neither in his budget speeches which, in this respect, are completely old-fashioned, nor in the Economic Survey, issued by the Lord President of the Council, is there any attempt made to examine, from this point of view, the necessities of the current position.

But while I am prepared to urge that this kind of policy is a policy of planning and indeed is the most important kind of planning which the state can undertake, I am not prepared to describe it as a policy of planning for full employment. This is not merely because of scruples about the statistical definition of full employment — although I always feel that the lay public might feel some justifiable bewilderment at the use of this term to cover a situation in which, by all except propagandist writers, it has been assumed that a substantial margin of unemployment would still continue to exist. My difficulty is rather that I think that there may easily arise situations leading to unemployment, which the stabilization of aggregate demand is unable itself to cure, although it may greatly ease whatever process of cure takes place. The changes, for instance, in the international conditions of supply and demand to which nearly every community is likely to be exposed, whatever its internal organization, will not necessarily exhaust themselves without occasionally causing structural unemployment; and we are surely raising false hopes if we claim that measures acting on over-all expenditure will prevent this kind of unemployment or cure it when it occurs.

Moreover, the promise of planning for full employment tends to elide rather too slickly the very real problems of wages policy. The theory of wages is not in a very satisfactory condition at the present day: we have still to reach unanimity about important matters concerning the general relationships between money wages and employment. But I think we are all in agreement that if, in a state of fairly high activity, there is a rise in the general level of wages, unaccompanied by a commensurate increase in productivity, then, either unemployment must develop, or there must be some degree of inflation. And this theoretical dilemma carries with it a corresponding dilemma for policy: in such circumstances are you to allow unemployment to develop, or are you to take steps which, if repeated, will involve a continued depreciation of the value of savings?

On this problem I am not prepared at present to adopt a very hard and fast position. Some of my friends who used to tell me I was a very perverse fellow indeed, when I ventured to suggest that sometimes trade union policy could be a bit of a nuisance, now tell me that I should go all out for a central wages policy and an entire transformation of the present apparatus of collective bargaining. This seems to me to be a serious step to take in a hurry; and I am still prepared to wait a little and see how trade union policy actually develops in conditions in which there are adequate safeguards against the danger of monetary deflation. But of one thing I am fairly sure, namely, that no government which has any interest in the position of small savings and the recipients of pensions and social insurance contributions could commit itself to a policy which involved a continuing wage inflation. I prefer, therefore, to frame my prescriptions for financial planning in terms which involve rather the attempt to maintain aggregate demand at a level which, *at current or slightly rising rates of wages*, would secure a reasonably high level of employment and utilization of resources. And I suspect that in a society, in which labour, at least, strongly objects to rigid controls from the centre, this may be the sort of norm which ultimately proves most acceptable.

Whatever happens about wages, the execution of such plans is not going to prove easy. If we are honest, we must admit that even now there are many things that we do not know about the dynamics of an expanding society, and, in the absence of complete knowledge, any policy of this sort is likely to prove something of a hit-or-miss business. Moreover, there are difficulties of politics and administration, both in the planning of public expenditure and in the manipulation of taxes and subsidies. When I went into the public service I admit I was surprised to discover the extent to which current expert discussion of the planning and timing of public investment had failed to affect either organization or thought within the machinery of government; and I am sure that there were and are still possibilities of improvement in that respect which offer great hopes for the future. But when human ingenuity has been stretched to the utmost, both in regard to organization and in regard to foresight, there will still remain the possibility of many mistakes and accidents. The timing of the best-laid plans may go wrong. The vicissitudes of democratic politics may impede the application of policies which in fact are necessary.

Hence, when I allow myself to speculate on these

matters, I come to be more and more impressed with the desirability of devising stabilizers which have a more automatic influence. I do not think that complete automatism is ever likely to be attainable. But I do believe that it should not be beyond the wit of man to think out mechanisms which shall be more independent of political and administrative accidents than investment and taxation policy. The suggestion in the Coalition White Paper on Employment Policy, of a certain automatic variation in contributions to social insurance, although doubtless exposed to many criticisms, seems to me to indicate a line on which further research is urgently needed. And if I may admit to what may prove to be the pursuit of an entirely false scent, I will confess that at times I have felt very interested in the suggestions, thrown out by Messrs. Frank and Benjamin Graham, for stabilizing the price level of certain storable commodities by a device which is essentially an extension of Marshall's symmetallism. If such a scheme were in fact administratively practicable on an international scale, I can see possibilities of mitigating world booms and slumps which certainly would be very attractive.

3. *Collectivism or Competitive Order*

I must not linger on this fascinating subject. Time presses and, before I close, I must try to fulfil my promise to say something, not only about the maintenance of

73

aggregate demand, but about the mechanism of relative demand and supply which has to operate within that envelope. What are we to say of the price and property system if aggregate demand is stabilized? What about the nationalization of the means of production, distribution and exchange?

This is clearly one of the greatest questions of the age; and it is most unlikely that even the most reasonable of men are going to reach final agreement about it in our lifetime — or, at any rate, not in mine, if in yours. But I should like to suggest, as I suggested at the end of my first lecture, that, serious as are the issues which are involved, we can discuss them in a much calmer frame of mind if, as I have endeavoured to do here, we approach them, having first examined our agreements and disagreements on other fundamental issues. If we are prepared to accept it as a general principle of policy that questions of distribution are best settled by direct operation on incomes and property, and that, given the distribution of incomes, where it is possible, the organization of production should be so directed as to meet the wishes of the citizens in their capacity as consumers; if we are in general agreement that, whatever the organization of production, it is desirable to keep steady the aggregate of money demand which that organization serves; if we agree on these assumptions, then, although momentous issues still remain unsettled, we have at least posed the problem of organization in a way in which it should be possible to discuss it without overmuch divagation into irrelevance.

Nevertheless, as I have said, we shall not agree quickly on these matters; and, in what I have still to say, I shall not pretend that agreement is likely. I shall simply try to set out a point of view which I do not expect you to accept but which I hope to make appear perhaps a little less imbecile than some of you may be in the habit of thinking it to be.

Now it is very clear that, even from the point of view of relative allocation, the price and private enterprise system is open to very grave strictures — at any rate if no deliberate attempt is made to curb its aberrations. There is no need for me, speaking here in Cambridge to an expert audience, to rehearse for your benefit a list of the ways in which, even under competitive conditions, there may arise divergencies between private and social net product. You will all be aware, too, of the good old infant industry argument which, in our day, beside its core of truth, has to provide the façade for so much that is either sinister or merely fanciful. And it would be otiose for me to dwell upon the various ways in which, when competition is limited and monopoly in any of its various forms is present, wealth may be spilt and progress retarded. I would like to add, however, that I am not one of those who believe that, were state intervention limited, monopoly would automatically disappear and effective competition take its place. It is true that much monopoly is the creation of policy. But, where freedom involves freedom to destroy freedom, I see no necessary self-preservative principle in competition; and at the present day, within the present legal framework, I think that much freedom has in fact been destroyed.

Confronted with these difficulties, it is obviously tempting to imagine a transfer of ownership and control to the state, or to an organ of the state, which would bring it about that the economic principle was observed and that, in every line of production, marginal cost was equal to price and the disharmonies of competitive or monopolistic production were automatically eliminated. If I thought this were at all probable, I would still be the collectivist I was when I began my career as a student of economics. If I could be convinced that, under such a system, consumer valuations would, in fact, set the target, that production would, in fact, be organized in a way which was likely to meet such criteria and provide for their more effective fulfilment as time went on, and that there would be no danger to the ultimate liberty of the individual — if I believed these things, I say, I do not think that the fact that I have sometimes argued against such a system in the past would prevent me from greeting its results with enthusiasm.

But, in fact, I am not yet persuaded. And, so far from my experience during the war having shaken my scepticism on these very essential points, I am afraid that it has deepened and confirmed it. I wish this were not so. I wish it were possible for me to share the hopes which inspire so many of my fellows. But this pleasure has not been vouchsafed me; and I must try to explain to you briefly the essential nature of my doubts.

First, I have little confidence in the acceptance, under general collectivism, of the criterion of consumers' valuations. I can well believe that on the hustings some lip service might be paid to the desirability of satisfying the consumer. But I find it difficult to believe that much attention would be paid to this in practice. When everything is complicated and difficult there is always a temptation to try to simplify the problem; I fear that under collectivism there would be many such temptations and that there would be a strong tendency to adapt the people to the plan rather than the plan to the people. I know many collectivists, whom I respect, who would repudiate this intention, who would proclaim their agreement with all that I said in my first lecture concerning the general objectives of production. But I suspect that they deceive themselves regarding the influences that would be operative. It is so easy for the machine to work the other way.

Even if this danger were not present as regards objectives, I should still have grave doubts as regards the working of the collectivist organization. I have studied with interest and respect the plans of Dr. Lange and Mr. Lerner for a collectivism based upon price calculations; and, although I have still some doubts as to the internal logic of their proposals, I recognize the ingenuity and sincerity with which they have tried to circumnavigate the difficulties of a purely centralized collectivism. But I cannot persuade myself that this is at all how collectivism is likely to work in practice. It is surely contrary to all that we know of the actual working of such systems which seem to tend, by a logic of their own, to organization in large blocks and to the issue of over-all directives. Surely much more probable than the decentralized semi-atomistic production units, guided solely by prices and costs, which are the essence of these proposals, is the organization of industries in giant corporations, exhibiting in an even heightened degree the rigidities of monopoly capitalism and little of its tendency, occasionally, to yield to outside pressure. When the state takes over production to-day, does it show any tendency whatever to pay regard to the requirements of the economic principle? Does it not rather tend to the consolidation of quasi-syndicalist blocks, unwilling even to reveal their accounts to the public and suppressing competition between their constituent parts even more remorselessly than the most predatory private mergers?

In this connection I cannot forbear from repeating to you the gist of a conversation which I once had, long before the war, with a leading collectivist who has now risen to a prominent position in the state. "Tell me, Robbins," he said to me, "what has been happening to this controversy about pricing in a socialist community? I have been a little out of touch recently, and I have not followed what has been going on." "Oh, much that is interesting has happened," I replied. "Your people, or most of them, have conceded the point about the difficulties of planning without prices. But they have staged a good debating come-back with some very interesting plans for restoring the price system without restoring

private property "; and, according to my lights, I gave
him a very sympathetic account of what were then the most
recent proposals of Mr. Lerner. The great man looked
very unhappy. " I have no use for that," he grumbled.
" That's not my idea of how to run industry. I want
industries organized as a whole so that " — and here he
waved expressive hands — " I can say to this industry
' You expand ', and to that industry ' You contract '."
I ask those of my colleagues who have worked in government offices during the war whether this does not reflect
a clearer picture of the probabilities of collectivist control
than all the elegant constructions of the so-called liberal
collectivists ?

But if this is so, I doubt very much concerning the
general efficiency of the system. You may say that one
should not worry overmuch about nice adjustments of
prices and marginal costs. I should not dissent from this
view — though it is sometimes expressed in very unex-
pected quarters. The important thing is not that at every
moment we should be in an exact state of ideal distribution
of resources, but that in a broad way there should be no
obstacles causing gross divergencies and that our organization should be such as to afford the maximum scope for
continual progress by way of cost reduction and innova-
tion. I find it difficult to believe that this state of affairs
is more likely to be achieved if competition and diffused
initiative are eliminated. There are doubtless many
checks on internal efficiency by way of cost accounting
which are available to public undertakings, and state-

79

aided research may render valuable service alike to public and private enterprise. But both as an incentive and a rough test of survival value, I do not know of any substitute for competition between independent units with a free field for new entrants. I know no evidence which shows that the suppression of competition in this sense promotes efficiency; I know much which suggests that in this way efficiency has been retarded. I confess that I find it more than a little paradoxical that at the present day we are continually told that in order to attain American standards of efficiency we must go over to wholesale collectivism.

But, beyond all this, I must confess to great fears regarding personal liberty under collectivism. Perhaps I have got things out of perspective. But I cannot get out of my head the conviction that there can be precious little freedom, precious little safeguard against arbitrary power, precious little spice and variety, in a society in which there is only one employer and only one property owner. In speculations of this sort it is a good rule to begin, at any rate, by making our imaginings as concrete and as close to our own experience as we can. I therefore often ask myself how much there would be left of academic freedom if all university appointments were controlled by one body. I think, too, of my life as a public servant. I had an almost uniquely fortunate position, with friendly ministers, the best chief in the world, good colleagues and opportunities of liberty and initiative which can have been the privilege of very few. But I have to recognize that I was seldom unconscious of that sense of unfreedom which comes from the knowledge that, if you fall out with your masters, there is no alternative way of doing what you want to do. I admire more than I can say that priestly caste, the administrative grade of the British Civil Service, whose anonymous self-sacrifice and devotion does so much to preserve order and efficiency in an otherwise disorderly scene. But I think that something quite essential would have gone out of life if we were all to become public servants in peace-time. I should fear this state of affairs as it would bear on the private life of the individual. I should fear, too, the consequences to political and cultural freedom.

For these reasons and for many others which I have not time here to relate, I am still inclined to hold that the goal of progress lies in a direction different from that of over-all collectivism. I am no foe to experiment; and I recognize that there are some fields where collectivist ownership and enterprise may have important functions to perform. But, as a general principle of organization, I prefer the diffused initiative and quasi-automatism which go, or can be made to go, with private property and the market. I believe that the loose institutions of individualism offer scope for the development of a way of life, more congenial to what most of us desire in our hearts, than the tight centralized controls which are necessary if these institutions are greatly curtailed or suspended.

This is no doubt a very unpopular and unfashionable

conclusion and I would summon to my aid the most powerful support I can muster. May I recall to your memories the passage in which, with all that incomparable magic of exposition which he, and he alone, of our generation could command, Lord Keynes set forth what he described as the traditional advantages of individualism. It is on page 380 of the *General Theory*.

" Let us stop for a moment ", he says, " to remind ourselves what these advantages are. They are partly advantages of efficiency — the advantages of decentralization and of the play of self-interest. The advantage to efficiency of the decentralization of decisions and of individual responsibility is even greater, perhaps, than the nineteenth century supposed; and the reaction against the appeal to self-interest may have gone too far. But, above all, individualism, if it can be purged of its defects and its abuses, is the best safeguard of personal liberty in the sense that, compared with any other system, it greatly widens the field for the exercise of personal choice. It is also the best safeguard of the variety of life, which emerges precisely from this extended field of personal choice, and the loss of which is the greatest of all the losses of the homogeneous or totalitarian state. For this variety preserves the traditions which embody the most secure and successful choices of former generations; it colours the present with the diversification of its fancy; and, being the handmaid of experiment as well as of tradition and of fancy, it is the most powerful instrument to better the future."

This does not imply, as Keynes would have been the first to argue, an attitude which is in the least content with letting things stay as they are; it is an attitude which is perfectly compatible with a redistribution of income and wealth which would have seemed the end of the world to our fathers; it is an attitude which essentially demands adequate action to maintain reasonably stable the volume of aggregate demand within which the system of markets and enterprise has to function. Nor, within the context of the operation of the market forces, does it imply any blind belief in the existence of economic harmonies; I have argued already that, within the present framework of law and institutions, I see no guarantee of good results from the free play of private interest. It does imply, however, the belief that, rather than to proceed by destroying the market and enterprise system, it is better to proceed by trying to improve it. It implies that, rather than stake all on the dubious prospects of over-all collectivism, it is better to retain existing mechanisms, but to erect around them, so to speak, a system of laws and institutions within which they may be made to work the right way. It implies, that is to say, a belief, not in a spontaneously harmonious free enterprise, but rather in a deliberately constructed competitive order.

This idea of a competitive order is by no means a simple notion. It is not just trust-busting — although there are many " trusts " which I should like to see bust. It involves the systematic revision of the whole apparatus of law and order — the law relating to patents, the law relating to restraint of trade, the law relating to limited liability and corporations, and many other branches of the law — with a view to creating conditions which tend to maintain effective competition, where it is technically possible, and to control monopoly in the public interest where technical conditions make monopoly inevitable. It involves the search for new methods of fiscal control, not only for the purpose of stabilizing aggregate demand, but also for the purpose of correcting and supplementing the operation of the incentive of relative prices, where analysis discloses the probability that this incentive works badly.

This is no light task. It would be idle to pretend that we yet possess the knowledge or the technique to proceed very far on our way. Much more work needs to be done, not only in the field of pure analysis but much more in the examination of the actual facts of industrial and commercial structure. Great as has been the progress of economics in other connections in recent years, this part of our subject has remained relatively undeveloped; the harvest is likely to be great, but the labourers in the field are few. In the excitement of perfecting our instruments of analysis we have tended to neglect the study of the framework which they assume. There is an urgent need for the best minds of the rising generation to apply themselves to this task of institutional invention in the light of patient, realistic investigations. Moreover, it is a mode of approach which is essentially unsensational. It lacks the appeal of the spectacular redemptionist solutions. A small change in the wording of the law may release the energies of thousands. But it is not a matter about which the man in the street, seeking, as ever, the universal solvent, is likely to get excited.

But it is not an impossible task. I see no objective factors in the situation which rule out the possibility of such developments. The belief that there are broad historic forces which drive us willy-nilly in one direction rather than the other, independent of our thoughts and wishes, seems to me based on misapprehension — an evil figment, misbegotten, in the swamps of the mind, by masochism on gullibility. The alleged inevitability of the competitive system to destroy itself is surely a matter of faith rather than of reason. There is nothing inevitable in the decision of the courts which makes it possible for a firm to organize a boycott of its competitors. There is nothing inevitable in the evolution of the law which permits fictitious personalities, in the shape of joint-stock companies, to enjoy the privilege of limited liability in respect of property in other companies. There is nothing inevitable in the conditions on which patent rights are granted. If these things were different, the resulting economic phenomena would be different. The fact that they are not different is not due to some mystical influence of the invention of the steam engine; it is due to the fact that people have thought that they should be as they are, or that perhaps it has not occurred to them that it would be possible for them to be different. In this respect, as in many others, our fates are more in our hands than we are apt to suppose. The policies which I have set forth in these lectures may be acceptable or they may be unacceptable — much as I have tried to be clear and provocative, I am not prepared to be dogmatic about that. But if they do commend themselves, then, as I see it, there is nothing in the nature of the world which prevents their being made the basis of action.

THE END

PRINTED BY R. & R. CLARK, LTD., EDINBURGH